COASTAL CROSSWINDS

An Evolution of Coastal Cooking

PYE THERIOT

First edition

ISBN: 979-8-90329-194-6

PART I

Caribbean Shores

The Careenage — Bridgetown, Barbads

Caribbean Coastal Traditions

MOVEMENT ARRIVES BEFORE CERTAINTY

At the edge of the harbor, boats come and go without schedule. Some arrive full, others light. Crates are unloaded quickly, not lingered over. Fish glint briefly in the shade before hands take over, cleaning, splitting, sorting while the air is still cool enough to allow choice. No one asks what will be cooked tonight. The question is what must be decided now.

Markets form around what survives. Pineapples bruised at the edges are moved first. Greens are separated by how long they will hold. A woman tastes salt between her fingers, then presses it into flesh already yielding to heat. Nothing here waits for hunger to explain itself. The work happens early, while options still exist.

Meals assemble themselves from movement. Ingredients are swapped without comment. What mattered yesterday may not arrive today. What arrives today may not arrive again soon. A dish takes shape once, then loosens. It travels, adapts, and returns changed.

Over time, movement leaves traces.

Some choices repeat not because they are taught, but because they continue to work. Fish are still split early. Fruit is still moved before it softens too far. Salt is still pressed into flesh while heat is gathering but has not yet claimed the day. No one marks these acts as tradition. They persist because they remain useful.

What changes is the speed of recognition. Decisions come sooner. Less is lost. Fewer corrections are required later. The work feels lighter, not because conditions have improved, but because attention has learned where to arrive first.

Even as routes shift and supplies change, this pattern holds. Food is treated as something that may be asked to travel again. What cannot last is shared. What might last is changed early, while time still offers options.

In places shaped by passage, continuity does not come from preservation alone. It comes from knowing when to act, and from acting before urgency arrives.

Creole Crescent

Harbor & Market - New Orleans

Louisiana • The Mississippi

St. Louis Cathedral

MOVEMENT NARROWS AS IT ARRIVES INLAND

Here, arrival gains rhythm. What comes today is likely to return tomorrow, and that expectation changes behavior before the stove is lit. Markets feel steadier. Storage replaces urgency. Ingredients are handled with an eye toward return rather than disappearance.

Bones are set aside without discussion. Fat is rendered, cooled, and saved. A pot is topped off before it is empty. Flavor deepens by repetition, not force. What was learned yesterday is tested again today, adjusted slightly, then trusted.

Cooking slows without stopping. Decisions are deferred on purpose. Heat is lowered and allowed to hold. The cook listens for change instead of forcing it. Action arrives smaller and quieter because it arrives earlier.

Movement still exists, but it has been compressed. Ingredients arrive bearing memory, and the kitchen learns how to hold that memory without fixing it in place.

With repetition, confidence settles in.

The same gestures return day after day. A pot is set on the stove without announcement. Bones are added when space allows. Fat is saved because it always has been. These acts no longer feel deliberate. They feel inevitable.

Time begins to compress around familiar rhythms. The cook no longer wonders how long something will take. Heat is lowered early. Waiting becomes part of the work rather than a pause between actions. Decisions arrive quietly, shaped by memory rather than urgency.

Mistakes become rarer, not because the work is simpler, but because attention arrives earlier. Small signals are noticed before they demand response. Adjustments shrink. Confidence grows without display.

In this narrowing, something important changes. Cooking no longer reacts to arrival alone. It anticipates return. What is done today is done with tomorrow in mind, not as preparation, but as continuity.

Southern Shores

Harborfront Market — Charleston, South Carolina

Lowcountry Coastal Traditions

MOVEMENT FINALLY RESTS

Land and water cooperate. Tides replace currents. Marsh replaces open passage. What arrives is expected to stay. Cooking responds by settling into care rather than urgency.

Meals return in familiar form. The same greens are gathered in measured amounts. Rice is rinsed, soaked, and cooked without hurry. Nothing is rushed to prove itself. What matters is steadiness.

Heat is moderated early. Pots are set low enough to forgive distraction. Intervention becomes rare not from indifference, but from confidence. Knowing when not to act becomes as important as knowing when to begin.

Knowledge moves quietly. Techniques are passed forward without explanation. Hands learn by watching. Meals taste the same week after week, and that sameness is not failure. It is proof.

This is a cuisine built on continuity. Care is applied steadily rather than urgently. What was shaped by movement is now shaped by patience. Here, steadiness becomes visible over time.

Meals repeat without apology. The same greens appear in season. Rice is prepared the same way it has been before. Nothing feels unfinished. Nothing asks to be improved. The work has learned where to stop.

Care expresses itself through restraint. Less is added. Less is corrected. The cook intervenes rarely, not because the work is unattended, but because it has been set up to succeed on its own.

Knowledge passes quietly. No one names the reasons. Hands learn by following familiar motion. What matters is not explanation, but consistency. What endures is not novelty, but trust.

In places where movement has settled, continuity becomes its own measure of success. The work does not announce itself. It holds.

PART II

Slower Is Better

NOTHING IMPROVES BY BEING RUSHED INTO PLACE

The work begins by waiting. A pan warms fully before it is asked to perform. Oil spreads, then stills. Food meets heat only after both have settled. This pause is not hesitation. It is preparation.

When pace slows, fewer decisions are required. Moisture redistributes on its own. Structure begins to form without force. Adjustments arrive earlier, while restraint is still possible.

Speed disguises its costs early. Heat raised too quickly demands correction later. Stirring interrupts contact before it can matter. The work appears efficient, but attention is scattered.

Slowing restores perception. Time becomes a collaborator rather than an obstacle. Acting at the right moment requires less effort than reacting after structure has set.

Over time, the benefits compound.

What once felt like delay becomes anticipation. The cook no longer wonders whether waiting is correct. The pause is built in. Heat is set with confidence and left to do its work. Fewer adjustments are needed because fewer mistakes are made.

When speed intrudes, the contrast is immediate. Food tightens too quickly. Moisture leaves unevenly. Correction arrives late and loudly. The difference is not subtle. It is felt in the hands before it is tasted.

Slowness does not eliminate effort. It redistributes it. Work shifts earlier, where influence is greater. The cook interferes less later because the conditions were allowed to align from the beginning.

Cooking By Sight, Sound & Smell

BEFORE COOKING IS MEASURED IT IS SENSED

Attention moves close. The pan changes before anything is added. Oil loosens, then stills. Its surface reflects heat more clearly than a gauge.

Sound steadies when conditions are right. Too sharp signals excess. Too quiet signals delay. When food enters at the correct moment, the pan accepts it without protest.

Aroma moves first. Fat warms and releases scent before color shifts. Sugars announce themselves before they darken. When thresholds approach, smell changes direction quickly, offering warning without urgency.

These cues are constant. What changes is whether they are noticed early enough to act gently.

Cooking by sight, sound, and smell does not replace technique. It locates judgment before instruction.

Attention sharpens through use.

Signals that once seemed faint become unmistakable. The change in sound that marks readiness. The scent that signals a threshold approaching. The shift in surface that asks for restraint rather than action. None of this is memorized. It is recognized.

When attention drifts, the cost is immediate. A pan overheats. Aroma turns sharp. Texture hardens beyond recovery. These moments do not punish. They instruct.

Over time, fewer tools are consulted. Not because they are rejected, but because they confirm what is already known. Measurement follows perception rather than leading it.

The cook learns to trust what arrives quietly. Judgment forms before urgency appears.

Heat Is An Ingredient

HEAT COMMITS FIRST

Its presence is already shaping outcome. Moisture moves. Fibers tighten. Surfaces begin to set. Once applied, heat does not reconsider.

The most influential decisions happen before contact. Afterward, restraint matters more than intent. Stirring too soon interrupts structure. Waiting too long hardens it beyond recovery.

Heat rewards attention given early. When respected rather than managed, it shapes flavor and texture through timing rather than force.

Understanding heat as an ingredient changes how it is used. Influence gives way to cooperation.

Heat leaves no room for revision.

Once structure has tightened, it cannot be loosened without loss. Moisture that has escaped will not return. Fibers that have seized will not relax again. The lesson is repeated often enough to become clear.

With experience, the cook stops asking how much heat is needed and starts asking when. Timing replaces intensity. Early restraint proves more powerful than later correction.

When heat is treated as a collaborator rather than a force to be managed, outcomes stabilize. Texture improves. Flavor holds. The work feels less dramatic because fewer rescues are required.

Respect replaces control.

The Coastal Flavor Triangle

BALANCE APPEARS BEFORE IT IS NAMED

The dish begins to assemble itself. Salt disappears early enough to support without announcing. Fat carries flavor without dulling it. Acid waits until structure has formed, then shifts everything with a small correction.

When proportion holds, no element stands apart. Flavor feels complete because nothing is missing.

Imbalance reveals itself immediately. Correction works best when it arrives quietly, while structure remains flexible.

The triangle does not impose rules. It describes relationships. Attention maintains balance more effectively than measurement ever could.

Balance becomes intuitive with repetition.

The cook begins to sense when a dish will need correction long before it asks for it. Salt is added earlier and in smaller amounts. Fat is adjusted before weight accumulates. Acid arrives only when structure can accept it.

When balance is missed, the error announces itself clearly. Too much sharpness. Too much heaviness. Too much restraint. These moments are corrected not by addition, but by restraint the next time.

Over time, the triangle recedes from conscious thought. It becomes a background structure, guiding decisions without announcing itself. The dish holds together because attention has learned where to rest.

Pan Sauces From What's Left Behind

AFTER FOOD LEAVES THE PAN
THE WORK CONTINUES

The surface records what has already happened. Browned traces mark where contact held long enough to change. Rendered fat carries decisions already made.

When liquid enters, it does not create flavor. It releases it. Steam lifts memory back into motion.

Recovery deepens more than addition. What is gathered from what remains carries greater authority than anything added late.

Continuity lives here. The meal completes itself by remembering where it has been.

Memory proves reusable.

The pan remembers contact. Where heat held long enough to change something. Where patience was rewarded. What remains is not residue. It is record.

When liquid loosens what is left behind, it carries more than flavor forward. It carries the history of the meal. Nothing added late carries the same authority.

Over time, the cook learns to trust what remains. Recovery replaces invention. Continuity replaces novelty. The end of the meal becomes the beginning of the next decision.

The Coastal Kitchen Is A Mindset

CONDITIONS RARELY HOLD STEADY

The kitchen responds early rather than urgently. Availability shifts. Weather interrupts plans. Freshness narrows its window without warning.

This way of working extends beyond the stove. Waste diminishes. Timing improves. Care becomes habitual rather than performative.

The kitchen becomes less about control and more about participation. Attention replaces force. Restraint replaces correction.

A coastal kitchen does not seek perfection. It seeks alignment. What holds here is not place, but practice.

This way of working extends outward.

Waste diminishes not through effort, but through foresight. Timing improves because decisions arrive earlier. Care becomes habitual rather than intentional.

The kitchen grows less reactive. Fewer emergencies arise. Fewer corrections are required. What once demanded attention now proceeds quietly.

Over time, restraint becomes the dominant gesture. Not from limitation, but from understanding. The work holds because it has been allowed to.

What remains is not a set of rules, but a way of noticing. Alignment replaces control. Practice replaces explanation.

EPILOGUE

THE CARIBBEAN

SCAN HERE FOR AN AUDIO ENCORE

NEW ORLEANS

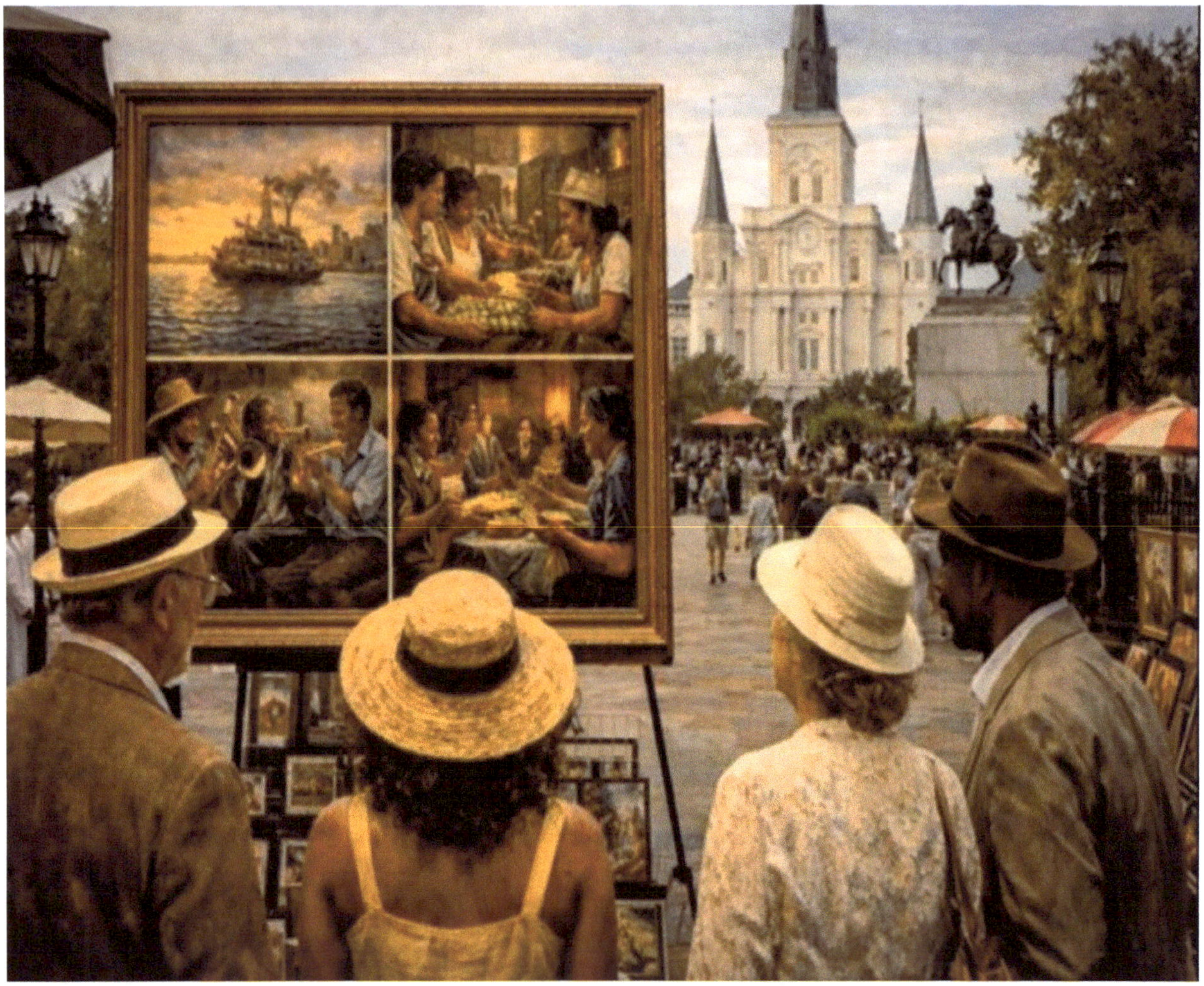

SCAN HERE FOR AN AUDIO ENCORE

CHARLESTON / LOW COUNTRY

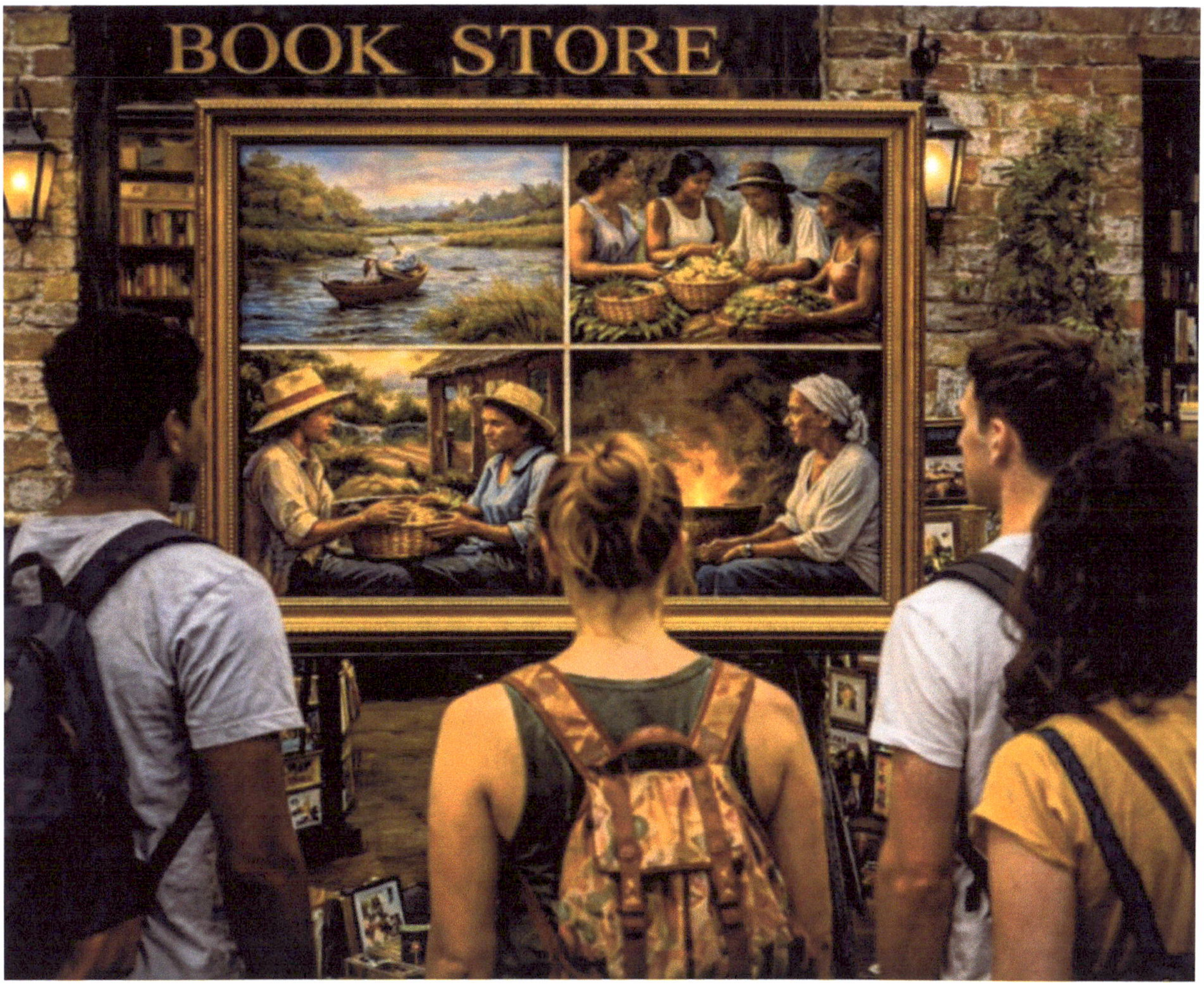

SCAN HERE FOR AN AUDIO ENCORE

Printed by Libri Plureos GmbH in Hamburg,
Germany

9 798903 291946